Jazz, Rags & Blues

8 original pieces for the late intermediate to early advanced pianist

MARTHA MIER

Jazz is an important and distinctive American contribution to 21st-century music. *Jazz, Rags and Blues,* Book 5, contains eight original solos that reflect the various styles of the jazz idiom. From the bright and happy sound of "Opening Night Jazz" to the slow blues swing style of "Blue Interlude," students will love the challenge of playing in the jazz style.

Jazz is fun to play! Students will be inspired and motivated by the syncopated rhythms and the colorful, rich harmonies of jazz—a style that has captured the imagination of performer and listener alike!

Alfred

ISBN-10: 0-7390-6051-1
ISBN-13: 978-0-7390-6051-3

Opening Night Jazz

Martha Mier

Spirited, with swing (♪♪ = ♩ ♪)

13
mf
16
f
19
mp
f
22
25
poco rit.

29
a tempo
mf
32
35
mp
mf
38
f
42
8va
p

for Julia Catherine Yarbrough

Memphis Blues

Martha Mier

Moderately slow, with swing

13
mp
mf
16
mp
mf
19
mp
23

26
mf
29
mp
mf
32
mp
mf
35
rit.
mp
8va

for Leighton Murri

HOT POTATO RAG

Martha Mier

Moderately (Play ♩♪ evenly)

18
mp
22
26
mf
30
f

34
mf
38
f
42
mf
46
f
50
mp
f

Steamboat Jazz

Martha Mier

Fast, with swing

17
mp
21
f
24
mf
28
mp
mf
31
mp
mf

35
mp
39
mp
f
43
mf
47
f
mf
51
molto rit.
mp

River City Blues

Martha Mier

With a slow, bluesy swing (♫ = ♩ ♪ triplet)

13
mp
17
mf
20
mp
mf
23
mp
27
mf
molto rit.
8va
mp

PERSNICKETY RAG

Martha Mier

Evenly, with a steady beat (Play ♫ evenly)

21
a tempo
mp
rit.
25
29
8va
mf
33
f
37
D.S. al Fine

Blue Interlude

Martha Mier

Slow, with swing

13
mf
17
mp
20
23
mf

26
29
32
35
molto rit.
8va
8va

Jazz Finale

Martha Mier

With excitement, in swing rhythm (♫ = ♩♪ triplet)

13
mf
16
mp
mf
19
22
f

26
a tempo
rit.
mp
30
34
mf
mp
f
38
molto rit.
p
8va

Alfred